"Theologically mind... role in my life, ...
my family, church, an... ...
effect.' Each of us is leaving a legacy of some sort;
Natalie Brand's life-giving book helps us see what that
legacy is and what it ought to be. With great precision
and warmth, Natalie gives us biblically compelling
reasons to crave God's doctrine and learn how to adorn
it with our lives. I'm excited to read this book with
other women."

**Bev Berrus**, Bible teacher; pastor's wife; contributing
author at *She Reads Truth*, *The Gospel Coalition*, and
*Well-Watered Women*

"*Priscilla, Where Are You?* is theologically rich and
heartwarmingly winsome, painting a captivating
vision for a church full of female theologians. Natalie
Brand writes that 'we have never needed Priscillas
more than we do today,' and the pages of this book
inspire us to this end, both in the example set by our
biblical heroine and indeed by the author herself.
I want my daughters and every woman in my church
to read this book so that they might be stirred to
'dig for gold' in God's Word—and thus to share this
treasure liberally with a theologically impoverished
world."

**Tim Blaber**, Pastor, Hope Church Winchester;
Director of Training for Commission Newfrontiers

"Priscillas, where are you? Natalie Brand calls for churches to be filled with Priscillas who rejoice in the treasure of knowing God. This is what every woman was created for. Natalie writes with warmth, wit, and clarity, leaving the reader with a hunger for theology. We hope local churches will pass out this book and women will read it with one another and grow."

**Keri Folmar**, Priscilla Talk, a podcast by 9Marks

"Natalie Brand urges all women to mine for the rivers of gold in God's Word and to become theologians rather than resting content with a superficial grasp of the truth. If every woman in every church was like the great Priscilla from the Bible, how much stronger and alive we all would be! And yet every woman can be, with encouragement from this gem of a book."

**Lee Gatiss**, Director of Church Society; author of *The Forgotten Cross: Some Neglected Aspects of the Cross of Christ*

"I love the straight talk in *Priscilla, Where Are You?* and its call to become women with 'gospel guts,' women who love and know the deep things of God. This brief but solid book is a winsome invitation to women to find our joy, our life, and our purpose in knowing, loving, and teaching the Scriptures."

**Nancy Guthrie**, Bible teacher; author of *Even Better Than Eden*

"Be inspired to dig for gold in God's Word, impacting the church and the world as you prize theology, share the truth, and shape others to praise God. 'Priscilla didn't need a pulpit to teach.' No one can read this book and minimise this inestimable privilege given to women today."

**Elinor Magowan**, Director of Women's Ministry, Fellowship of Independent Evangelical Churches (FIEC)

"Priscilla is a heroine for so many of us—a woman who worked hard, risked her life for the gospel, and raised others up in the faith. We love her. In this short book, Natalie Brand invites us to walk in Priscilla's footsteps, pursuing our Lord as Priscilla did two thousand years ago. This is an encouraging read— I appreciated Priscilla, my other sisters in the faith, and my Lord even more as I arrived at the last page."

**Jen Oshman**, Bible teacher; author of *Welcome: Loving Your Church by Making Space for Everyone*

"It's exciting to be a woman who loves God's Word; it holds life-transforming treasures. Priscilla knew that well, but we sometimes forget. How good, then, to be reminded in this little book of every Christian woman's call to learn, live, love, and pass on good theology. As Natalie Brand encourages us to see, doing so is a privilege and a joy."

**Helen Thorne**, Director of Training and Resources, Biblical Counselling UK

# PRISCILLA, WHERE ARE YOU?

## A Call to Joyful Theology

### Natalie Brand

*Priscilla, Where Are You? A Call to Joyful Theology*

© 2023 by Natalie Brand

www.UnionPublishing.org
Bridgend, Wales, United Kingdom

Cover design by Rubner Durais
Book designed and typeset by CRB Associates, Potterhanworth,
Lincolnshire

978-1-7397062-7-2 (paperback)
978-1-7397062-8-9 (eBook)

*Dedicated to the Priscillas in my life—*
*sisters with whom I have laughed, cried,*
*and worshipped*

"I had much to write to you,
but I would rather not write with pen and ink.
I hope to see you soon,
and we will talk face to face."
3 John 1:13–14

# Contents

# A Shout-Out

## All Christians Are God's Theologians

This book is a shout-out—like a mention from the DJ behind the decks or on the radio. It's a cry of admiration and gratitude to a woman whom we meet in the pages of the New Testament. I am not the first to give Priscilla (or "Prisca") a shout-out. The apostle Paul gives her and her husband several in his letters to the churches. "Greet Prisca and Aquila," he writes to the Romans, "my fellow workers in Christ Jesus, who risked their necks for my life, to whom not only I give thanks but all the churches of the Gentiles give thanks as well" (Rom. 16:3–4).[1] Priscilla was a woman who faithfully served the church in practical ways: she corrected theology, hosted the local church in her home, committed herself to evangelism, and even saved the apostle Paul's life! Paul is right; the church *is* indebted to her.

Yet in many ways Priscilla was no different from you and me. Sure, she made it to the pages of the

---

1 See also 1 Corinthians 16:19; 2 Timothy 4:19.

Bible and was a friend and colleague of Paul. Still, it was her simple commitment to gospel truth that proved her to be indispensable to the church. She was a woman with a God-glorifying appetite for theology, seeing no disconnect between *loving* God and *knowing* about him. Her legacy, then, is one we can also enjoy. Like Priscilla, we can be theologians who carefully and competently handle the gospel of truth.

While many of us would never actually give ourselves the label "theologian," the Puritan John Owen said, "*All* true Christians are God's theologians."[2] What is theology? It is the study of God by Christian men, women, and children. It is our pursuit of knowledge of God. And it is only possible because the living God has revealed himself. If you are a Christian, then you are God's theologian. And only those who believe in God can grow in knowledge of him. Owen affirms that if we do not love God, we are outsiders to theology.[3] How can we behold anything of God when we are dead in faith and have no love for him?

---

2 John Owen, *Biblical Theology: The History of Theology from Adam to Christ*, trans. Stephen P. Westcott (Pittsburgh: Soli Deo Gloria, 1994), 687. Emphasis added.

3 Owen, *Biblical Theology*, xlvi.

Therefore, *theology is solely and uniquely the concern of the Christian.*

## A Call

This book isn't just a tribute to a woman who lived two thousand years ago. It is a call to Christian women today. It is a cry for the Priscillas of all ages, ethnicities, and educations to come forth! Here is a sinner saved by grace who loved the Lord her God with all her heart, with all her soul, with all her mind, and with all her strength.[4] As the chaos of secular culture intensifies and presses hard against the church, we have never needed Priscillas more than we do today.

Perhaps you disagree and think you don't need to study doctrine—that is, the beliefs and teachings of the Bible. "We don't need theology. We just need Jesus!" was the reply a friend of mine received from his ministry director when he asked him for a statement of faith. What a sham! What a contradiction! Isn't the statement "we just need Jesus" nothing but baseline theology itself? It's a beautiful, simple confession of faith—a declaration of Christ's unique sufficiency! Can we say anything about Jesus without

---

4  See Matthew 22:37; Mark 12:30; Luke 10:27; Deuteronomy 6:5.

asserting our theology? Even those who use his name as an expletive betray their theological position of blasphemy, ridicule, or unbelief.

Doctrine is the flesh and bones of our faith. Have you ever wanted to explain a Christian belief but found your mouth dried up as all the relevant Bible verses evaporated from your head? I sure have. And many of us know those cold waves of uncertainty and doubt that wash over us as we answer the tricky questions: "Why *did* Jesus need to die? *Can* we lose our salvation? How, exactly, is God three-in-one?"

Donald Macleod says, "We can never bear effective personal witness unless we know what the gospel actually is."[5] This is why the book of Hebrews calls us beyond a token theology of Christ: "Therefore let us leave the elementary doctrine of Christ and go on to maturity" (Heb. 6:1). The Lord has a desire for every one of his people to reach a mature understanding of who he is and why he is sufficient for salvation. Jesus wants us to dive hungrily into his Word and grow in it. This is why Owen says Christians are *God's* theologians, because the Lord wants this for us. He has designed and created us to pursue

---

5 Donald Macleod, *A Faith to Live By: Understanding Christian Doctrine* (Fearn, Ross-shire, Scotland: Christian Focus, 2010), 9.

truth about him. He has given us a powerful, trainable muscle in our heads so we can drive the sharp end of our intellect into knowing him.

Therefore, we all need theology, because *truth about God and the gospel fortifies the Christian.*

Priscilla is a model for us in this; she devoted herself to pursuing truth. We know that because when it was needed, she was able to explain the things of God "more accurately" (Acts 18:26). In these things you too can grow in knowledge and confidence—for the sake of those you love who don't believe; for the sake of your local church family; for the sake of your worship of God and enjoyment of Christ.

Whether you are a lover of the Word and biblical doctrine, or completely overwhelmed, or theologically malnourished, I hope this book will spur you on in knowing God. These pages do not include "Five Quick Steps to Theological Maturity" (as if there were such a thing!). Besides, we all have different capacities and responsibilities, and the Lord works in us differently. This book is simply *a call* to *treasure* God-truth (or doctrine) and *pursue* the gracious gift we have in theology.

To know God is to love him.

## Chapter One

# Priscilla's Legacy

Priscilla and her husband first appear in the pages of the New Testament in Acts 18 as they connect with the apostle Paul in the streets of Corinth and join gospel forces with him. By this time, Paul is on the last leg of his second missionary journey. He has been to many places since he left Jerusalem: he has travelled up to Syria, crossed the land mass of modern-day Turkey, entered Macedonia, and later, due to "babbling" the gospel in the marketplace, has been invited to address Athens' famous hill of speakers, the Areopagus (Acts 17:18–19). Here Priscilla enters the story:

> After this Paul left Athens and went to Corinth. And he found a Jew named Aquila, a native of Pontus, recently come from Italy with his wife Priscilla, because Claudius had commanded all the Jews to leave Rome. And he went to see them, and because he was of

the same trade he stayed with them and worked, for they were tentmakers by trade.

(Acts 18:1–3)

We don't know whether Paul hunted Priscilla and Aquila down because an acquaintance had informed him of them, or if they just happened to meet in Corinth's synagogue or through the tentmaking trade. Either way, this was a significant meeting. From this time on, the three of them live, work, and minister together for at least a year and a half, forming a trio of tents, theology, and evangelism (see Acts 18:11, 18).

Oh, to be a fly on the wall as they worked their knives, awls, and burnishers—as they cut, trimmed, and bevelled, stitching coats, awnings, and pavilions! Can you imagine the conversations? Paul no doubt shared his Damascus Road experience (Acts 9:1–9). He probably told Priscilla how Lydia had come to Christ on the banks of the river in Philippi (Acts 16:13–15) and that singing worship songs in the prison there led to a supernatural earthquake and the jailer turning to Christ (vv. 25–40). He may have told her of his preaching in Thessalonica and of how Greeks and "not a few of the leading women" were persuaded (Acts 17:4), or about the Bereans who were so hungry for truth that they ravenously pored over the Scriptures to check whether Paul and Silas's teachings were true. Subsequently, "Many of them therefore believed, with not a few Greek women of high standing as well as men" (v. 12).

Priscilla, Aquila, and Paul shared warm times of fellowship together, feeding each other with the Old Testament Scriptures—from their memories and their scrolls. They probably had heated debates in the evening over the first-century Corinthian equivalent of hot chocolate with squirty cream. I am sure every conversation was a treat!

We can imagine Priscilla standing up from the table and moving to the doorway to enjoy the cool evening breeze—storing up the apostle's accounts of sinners being transformed by the gospel, her heart overwhelmed, humbled that God would use her in the building of his church. Her face is displaying a stomach-stirring desire to speak out the gospel… I know what that looks like. I have seen it on the faces of many dear sisters in Christ: a holy restlessness to declare aloud the goodness and wonders of God.

## Neck-Risker with Gospel Guts

What was Priscilla like? Scripture doesn't give many details. We don't know, for instance, whether or not she and her husband had any children. We do know that she was living in a foreign land. Luke explains that Priscilla and Aquila had recently come from Italy "because Claudius had commanded all the Jews to leave Rome" (Acts 18:2). This makes Priscilla a refugee, forcefully uprooted from her home simply because the emperor believed Christians were troublemakers. She was a Jewish Christian who had experienced anti-Jewish and anti-Christian prejudice. She knew the taste of persecution. One commentator writes, "Leaving Rome under such circumstances must have been a great trial for those concerned, but Luke shows how, in God's providence, the coming of this couple to Corinth, and then Ephesus, advanced the work of the gospel significantly."[1]

Although Prisca may mean "old woman" and Priscilla "little old woman," she was no mouse! Priscilla was a woman with gospel guts. Throughout the span of the New Testament, we see her moving between Rome, Corinth, Ephesus, and back again, finally settling in Rome after the death of Claudius. It seems that wherever she was, Priscilla was intentional in sharing the good news of Christ. And in

---

1 David G. Paterson, *The Acts of The Apostles* (Grand Rapids: Eerdmans, 2009), 508.

whatever country her home stood, she opened it wide to Christ's beloved bride, the church.

Paul's most significant shout-out to our couple is at the end of the book of Romans: "Greet Prisca and Aquila, my fellow workers in Christ Jesus, who risked their necks for my life, to whom not only I give thanks but all the churches of the Gentiles give thanks as well" (Rom. 16:3–4). Paul boasts in Priscilla and Aquila because they loyally stuck their necks out for him. We are not told more than that. We can only guess when this took place. There was some ugly opposition to their evangelism after the trio met in Corinth (see Acts 18:5–6). The Lord nonetheless spoke to Paul in a vision and told him to persevere (vv. 9–10). Later, Corinth's leading Jews attacked Paul and brought him to a tribunal, escalating into an angry mob beating the synagogue ruler (vv. 12, 17). However, it is more likely that Priscilla and Aquila's rescue of Paul involved jumping into the pandemonium of the later riots in Ephesus (Acts 19:23–41), an incident Paul describes as fighting with "beasts" (1 Cor. 15:32). In all of this, it is obvious that Priscilla and Aquila are "a couple with real backbone," as my friend Sharon Mac has expressed it.[2]

---

2 Sharon McClaughlin Wilmshurst, "Theology That Leaves a Legacy," Union Women Advent Conference, December 13, 2021.

## Truth-Teacher

Saving Paul's life is not the extent of Priscilla's legacy, however, as we saw earlier. It is not until the trio take a ship to Ephesus and then part ways, Paul continuing to Syria, that we witness Priscilla's real gospel legacy (Acts 18:18–21). Luke somewhat surprisingly pulls us back to Ephesus, where Priscilla and Aquila now are, minus Paul:

> Now a Jew named Apollos, a native of Alexandria, came to Ephesus. He was an eloquent man, competent in the Scriptures. He had been instructed in the way of the Lord. And being fervent in spirit, he spoke and taught accurately the things concerning Jesus, though he knew only the baptism of John. He began to speak boldly in the synagogue, but when Priscilla and Aquila heard him, they took him aside and explained to him the way of God more accurately.
>
> (Acts 18:24–26)

Enter Apollos, a North African Jew named after the Greek god of the sun. Apollos is a bold and articulate communicator. We are told he has been "instructed in the way of the Lord" (v. 25). So it is safe to assume

12

he knew well the saving life, death, and resurrection of Jesus. Apollos was no rookie: he knew his Bible (v. 24) and preached the gospel both passionately and "accurately" (v. 25). But his theology was incomplete. He "knew only the baptism of John," a baptism of repentance. Apollos hadn't been told how the Lord Jesus had fulfilled and superseded John's baptism. He was not yet aware of the full Christian baptism, in the name of the Father, Son, and Holy Spirit, given by Christ himself in the Great Commission (Matt. 28:19).

So, what do Priscilla and her husband do? "When Priscilla and Aquila heard him, they took him aside and *explained to him the way of God more accurately*" (v. 26). They filled the holes in his theology. They brought him up to speed in his gospel understanding. Sure, they were not eloquent in public speaking like Apollos. Priscilla and Aquila were street artisans; they did not have Apollos's learning. Nevertheless, their theology was sufficiently thorough that when they heard even a persuasive communicator speak error, they knew it—even if that error was a gap in theology. They knew the important role of baptism in God's saving work. They didn't heckle. They didn't boo. They quietly took Apollos aside and discipled him.

If she were alive today, I think Priscilla would be slipping meaty Christian books into the hands of her church siblings and posting the Nicene Creed on her Instagram account. She would be the one asking important questions after church services and, while sipping tea and coffee, feeding her brothers and sisters with Christ. Taking time to correct Apollos demonstrates Priscilla's fearless love and concern that the church of Christ should mature and grow in truth. Something momentous happened in her and Aquila's encounter with Apollos. It was so much more than a quick word in private. Otherwise, why would Luke have bothered to include it in his account? In this seemingly small act, Priscilla bequeaths the whole church a profound legacy.

You may ask why I do not attribute this legacy more to Aquila—but this is not a book about Aquila. And Priscilla's name comes before that of her husband in Luke's account (see v. 26), perhaps emphasising that she was the more vocal teacher. Some say this might be because she was from a more prestigious family. Either way, Priscilla was a teacher of God-truth.

## Priscilla's Protection

We are going to linger here, loitering in the corridor with Priscilla, Aquila, and Apollos, so to speak, in order that we can truly appreciate Priscilla's gift to Apollos and the church. At this point, however, I want to characterise it in one word: *protection*. With Aquila, Priscilla offers Apollos profound protection. Jonathan Leeman explains:

> There [has] never [been] a shortage of serpentine or beastly attacks against the church. Every woman, therefore, should desire to be equipped for the work of the ministry of building up the body of Christ … *Every woman needs rock-solid doctrine. Imagine if every woman in your church had it. What kind of protection do you think that would afford your church?*[3]

Priscilla's gift to the church is her rock-solid doctrine. Because of this, she gave an up-and-coming preacher, and the precious newly formed church, theological correction. Sure, Priscilla protected the apostle Paul from the "beasts" of Ephesus, putting her life on the line for him. But this is nothing compared to the protection she gave Apollos from

---

3 Jonathan Leeman, "Essential and Indispensable: Women and the Mission of the Church," 9marks, 9marks.org, December 20, 2019. Emphasis added.

deficient theology: from such theology men and women have slid into error and then blasphemy. It is not a long journey from there to justifying our sin, backsliding, and complete unbelief or apostasy. In theological error, we find the lies of Satan and our own spiritual decline and decay. Is it not naive of us, then, to neglect strengthening our skills in doctrinal truth? Aren't we told to "fear him who can destroy both soul and body in hell" (Matt. 10:28)? Oh, how Satan must love shoddy theology!

You see, there was another Priscilla—one who lived in the year AD 170 in Phrygia. She too belonged to a trio, working with a man called Montanus and a woman named Maximilla. They too had great influence. Believing themselves to be possessed by the Holy Spirit (a "gift" that, incidentally, they claimed wasn't available to others), this trio supposedly brought the church into a new era of prophecy and revelation. Their heretical movement is now known as Montanism. In their misinterpretation of Scripture and heretical legacy, instead of building up a young man in orthodoxy, they confused the theologian Tertullian. You can do your own research on this trio of theological troublemakers. Suffice it to say: they didn't rightly handle the Word of God.

How different the legacy of this later Priscilla was from that of our own! And the gifts these two women gave to the church couldn't be more dissimilar: one a gift of orthodoxy, the other of heresy.

Our Priscilla knew that treasuring the gospel meant safeguarding your brothers and sisters in Christ. This is why God gives us teachers and leaders:

> To equip the saints for the work of ministry, for building up the body of Christ, until we all attain to the unity of the faith and of the knowledge of the Son of God ... so that we may no longer be children, tossed to and fro by the waves and carried about by every wind of doctrine. (Eph. 4:12–14)

Priscilla cared enough to correct. She understood that cracks and crannies in our knowledge of God and his gospel are dangerous weaknesses, prone to split open eventually, with devastating results. Priscilla and Aquila sought to protect Apollos from blunders because they knew that theology fortifies the Christian, and theology fortifies the church.

17

Priscilla is a woman of whom we see only a glimpse in the New Testament, but she is a true heroine.

*Where are you today, Priscilla? You were not contentious. You saw no reason to enter a power struggle with the men with whom you ministered. You were not jealous of Paul's ministry or Apollos's gifts. Instead, you sought the good of the body. You served your brothers in Christ, putting your life on the line for one and carving out time to teach the other. You were a woman of gospel guts. A neck-risker. A teacher of truth.*

*For this, we thank you!*

# FAITH

*But recall the former days when, after you were enlightened, you endured a hard struggle with sufferings, sometimes being publicly exposed to reproach and affliction, and sometimes being partners with those so treated.* (Heb. 10:32–33)

1. Priscilla was a woman of faith. How is this evident in the things we know about her? Read Acts 18 and identify several examples.

2. Why do you think Luke, the author of Acts, momentarily pans away from Paul to include this story in his account? Why is this episode so important? What does it demonstrate in the life of the church?

3. John Calvin once said that Priscilla and Aquila passed through many troubles, by the Lord's hand, so that they might more "greedily" receive the grace of God's redemption. He said that in this they were ready students, submitting themselves to be taught whatever the Lord wanted to teach them.[4]

---

4 John Calvin, *Commentary upon the Acts of the Apostles*, vol. 2 (Calvin Translation Society, 1844), 181.

How can we turn our sufferings into an opportunity to grab hold of God's grace and learn the lessons he has for us? Who models this for us in Scripture?

4. In what way did Priscilla correct Apollos? What do you think contributed to her ability and willingness to do so?

5. John Owen said, "All true Christians are God's theologians, as the saving light of the gospel has been bestowed upon them all."[5] What do you think he meant? What are the implications of this for daily life?

---

5 Owen, *Theology*, 687.

## Chapter Two

# Digging for Gold

Once, two brothers lived in a tiny miners' cabin on the side of a mountain. Much about the brothers was the same: they spoke the same way, dressed in the same clothes, ate the same food, and each slept on an equally creaky cot. They each worked tirelessly every single day, from sunrise to sundown, except on Sundays, when they washed in an old tin tub and wrote supply lists with pencil stubs.

Although the brothers had mined together for many years, they did not share the same heart for mining. Whilst the elder one was a proficient prospector—dredging, sluicing, and panning the surrounding creeks and rivers with skill and dedication—the younger brother wanted more. He was not satisfied with flakes and nuggets. His heart longed for rivers of gold etched into the ore. And every day he was plagued by the realisation that attainable treasure coursed under his feet.

So he dug. And he dug deep! By the dim light of one brass lamp, he tunnelled one hundred feet, then two hundred feet, and finally three hundred feet into the mountain. At first he found streaks of dust, and then he uncovered veins of gold running through the rock. In anticipation, he laboured on, until, after much toil, he found gold beyond compare.

Theology is mining. It is digging deeply into God's mighty Word to find rivers of gold—rivers that declare God's attributes, the splendour of his glory, the mystery of a three-persons-in-one God, and the mighty generosity of his salvation in Christ. Theology is a tool brandished by faith-filled men, women, and children to delve into the things of God. It is the pick or the trowel with which we forage God's self-revelation. And the fact that God invites us to do this is all of grace.

But many of us are like the older brother, staying on familiar ground at a depth where we are proficient and comfortable. Our desire extends only to paddling in the shallows, and we have a view of God that reflects this. We think we know it all, or we choose to play it safe. Satisfied with the same Bible passages, we turn to them time and again, while other pages are never ruffled or rumpled. We say the same prayers and read the same types of Christian books. We never strike out for new territory. We never dive into the depths. Is it surprising, then, that we sometimes get spiritually bored?

The younger brother's hunger is a better picture of what the appetite of the Christian should be. Theology isn't just for pastors, academics, or Bible translators. Priscilla knew this. As we have seen, *all* Christians are God's theologians. This is *why* we should dig. Deeply.

But there are other questions too. *Where* should we dig? Doesn't theology mean reading books written by dead guys? And how do we know when we've struck gold? We will answer all these questions in this chapter. But thankfully, theology has a basecamp: God's own self-revelation. And this is our starting point.

## Theology's Basecamp

What we believe about God is the single most important thing about us.

This is an understatement. What we believe about God is our life or death; our heaven or hell; our past, present, future, and eternity. But God doesn't leave us to seek him out by ourselves. One theologian has said, "With all his searching, man has not been able to find out for himself the deepest things of God."[1] God is beyond the grasp of mere human reason or ingenuity.

At the beginning of time, as Adam lay newly formed in the dust, any hope of him enjoying a relationship with his Creator rested upon God himself. He had to reveal himself. But our God is a self-revealing God. In fact, the God of the Bible has gone to great lengths to make himself known.

### Beetles, Buffalo, and Badgers

First, the Lord has revealed himself in the glories and wonders of his creation. Psalm 19 tells us that all of creation roars in standing ovation to the power of our God. "The heavens declare the glory of God, and the sky above proclaims his handiwork" (v. 1). But creation exhibits not just his *power*, but his very *nature*—what God is like. Paul writes, "For his invisible attributes, namely, his eternal power and divine nature, have been clearly perceived, ever since the creation of the world, in the things that have been made. So [the ungodly] are without excuse" (Rom. 1:20).

---

1 Benjamin B. Warfield, *Biblical Doctrines* (Edinburgh: Banner of Truth, 1988), 133.

Indeed, how can we miss it? All the wonders of the natural world showcase the genius, animation, intricacy, colour, subtlety, order, extravagance, magnitude, and wealth of their Creator. Every step of the beetle and every stomp of the buffalo announce their Maker. This is the doctrine of general revelation. "Day to day pours out speech, and night to night reveals knowledge" (Ps. 19:2), as creation asserts its Creator:

> The trees of the Lord are watered abundantly,
>     the cedars of Lebanon that he planted. ...
> The high mountains are for the wild goats;
>     the rocks are a refuge for the rock
>         badgers. ...
> O Lord, how manifold are your works!
>     In wisdom have you made them all;
>     the earth is full of your creatures.
>
> (Ps. 104:16, 18, 24)

Gawping at the delicious beauty of the world around us—the millipede's legs, the audacious dance of the bird of paradise, the silver belly of the white poplar leaf, the haughty beard of the iris—is fundamental to our lives as God's theologians. As Augustine wrote, "All things animate or inanimate praise you through the lips of those who contemplate them."[2] When we glory in God's creation, we make public his holiness, goodness, and all the perfections of his character (Rom. 1:20). Remember this when you go out for your next walk. You are fulfilling *your* role as God's theologian.

### Messengers, Men, and Manuscripts

We know from the Old Testament that God has also revealed himself and his will by sending angelic messengers to his people—angels sent straight from the throne room of God, talking, eating, sharing God's purposes and plans with sinful humanity. And of course God interacted personally with Israel for many centuries by his human mouthpieces, the prophets: "Long ago, at many times and in many ways, God spoke to our fathers by the prophets" (Heb. 1:1).

Yet this was still not enough. So the Lord literally breathed out his Holy Word in the Scriptures (2 Tim. 3:16), disclosing himself by the power of the Holy Spirit in human letters scratched on scrolls. The Spirit of God employed, guided, and carried

---

2 Augustine, *Confessions*, trans. P. Burton (New York: Everyman's Library, 2001), 87.

the minds of the men who wrote. "For no prophecy was ever produced by the will of man, but men spoke from God as they were carried along by the Holy Spirit" (2 Pet. 1:21). In Scripture God divulges his very heart, from old covenant to new covenant, detailing his story of redemption for us to understand.

The Bible does not just speak of God's grace but is an awesome *demonstration* of it. We should call this to mind when we reach for the Bible as though it were merely our keys or our phone. We should not forget God's immeasurable mercy in preserving the Bible for us throughout the ages. Without it we would all be ships lost at sea, left to nothing but our own wild notions, idolatry, and despair.

## God Himself Comes

As if that were not enough, God then revealed himself most supremely in the miracle of the incarnation. "Long ago, at many times and in many ways, God spoke to our fathers by the prophets, but in these last days he has spoken to us by his Son, whom he appointed the heir of all things, through whom also he created the world" (Heb. 1:1–2). Ultimately, then, in his self-revelation, God doesn't send a man or a messenger—he comes himself in the Son, the Lord Jesus Christ. "He is the radiance of the glory of God and the exact imprint of his nature" (v. 3).

In the incarnation, God the Son took on human flesh and was found in the womb of a virgin. Is there no place that God Almighty *won't* go to reveal himself, if he graces the body of a young girl? In this, the second person of the Trinity—the Son— Jesus Christ comes … not just to reveal God, but he *himself* is the revelation.[3] In the incarnation we see that God is truly knowable as he makes himself fully known.

In no other faith has the divine gone to such extent to reveal himself. And in no other faith has the god revealed himself so entirely! This is why theology is uniquely the concern of the Christian, as we noted. In sharing himself with us, God invites us to become his theologians, because he wants his people to take hold of him. Theology, then, is no longer about books we can't lift, concepts we can't grasp, and words we can't pronounce. It is about grace: and it starts with a Creator bending down and sharing himself with his creation.

---

3 Robert Letham, *Systematic Theology* (Wheaton: Crossway, 2019), 62.

## *All* of God for *All* the People

I love the way that Scripture sometimes hits you between the eyes like a Davidic pebble. This happened to me recently while I was dipping into the book of Joshua. By this point in the story, Jericho has been razed, God has judged the family of Achan because Achan disobeyed God and stole from the Jericho booty, and Ai has just been captured by a sneaky ambush (chs. 6–8). Now, in chapter 8, Joshua wants to renew the covenant just as Moses had commanded (v. 33). So he gathers Israel between the same two mountains as Moses did earlier (Deuteronomy 27). All of Israel is there: the people, priests, elders, officers, judges, and any visitors who want in (such as the recently recruited Rahab mentioned in Joshua 6:25). The people are silent and expectant.

And what does Joshua do? He writes a copy of the law and reads it aloud. It was the author's repeated emphasis in the next two verses that struck me squarely in the forehead:

And afterward he read *all* the words of the law, the blessing and the curse, according to *all* that is written in the Book of the Law. There was not a word of *all* that Moses commanded that Joshua did not read before *all* the assembly of Israel, and the women, and the little ones, and the sojourners who lived among them. (vv. 34–35)

There was not a word Joshua did not read, and the law was read to *all* the people, not a select few. "Before *all* the assembly": this means not just the men, who would normally make up the roll call, but also the women, the little ones, and the Gentiles. Every single person was invited, because Joshua knew that the Word belonged to everyone!

The renewing of the covenant wasn't an exclusive tabernacle activity for just the priests and leaders. Even the three-foot cuties sucking their chubby thumbs belonged to the covenant community. If the covenant was going to be renewed, then the grubby toddlers had to be there too! The Word of God belongs to all.

Knowing God in his Word is the calling, even duty, of every believer. Priscilla's legacy also demonstrates that regardless of age, gender, race, education, and intellectual ability, the Word of God belongs to all. If Scripture is the basecamp of theology, then loving the Word and diving into biblical doctrine is one and the same thing. This means that books about our God are for the whole family: husband, wife, child, and visitor. They are *community resources*.[4] Their accessibility to all is one obvious way that we can centralise worship in the home.

This is why we need to bring our theological libraries out of the study and into the family room. Our commentaries and lexicons, our Puritan paperbacks and systematic theologies—shouldn't they belong to every member of the family? Everyone should be encouraged to dig deeper into God, engaging personally and practically with God's self-revelation. Through the Scriptures, the Spirit of Christ should be given full opportunity to work in every member of the family, to stir new faith in those who don't yet believe and more in those who do.

Theology is for the whole covenant community because we are "a chosen race, a royal priesthood, a holy nation" (1 Pet. 2:9). Here we hit upon the doctrine of *the priesthood of all believers. All of God for all the people!* This is why *all* Christians are God's theologians. This is another reason why faith alone makes a theologian.

## Gold!

The gold in theology is God himself. It is not the learning, the reading, or the books. It is certainly *not*

---

4 Thanks to my brother in Christ Justin Schell for this wording.

any reputation, profile, or platform one might receive. Our holy, awesome, triune God—Father, Son, and Holy Spirit—is the treasure in theology. We strike gold when we uncover something new of him and his gospel, something we didn't see coming, and get floored in wonder.

I have witnessed this amongst the women I have taught. Hearts soaring and minds buzzing, their vision of God has been broadened; they have apprehended more of him and found it truly exhilarating. And this has changed them forever. That is one thing I love about theology: unearthing more of who God is and his lavish gifts in Christ, as Benjamin Warfield says, brings you "into the very presence of God; his ways, his dealing with men, the infinite majesty of his Being … Put the shoes from off your feet in this holy presence!"[5]

Warfield leads us to another point. Theology isn't just learning biblical facts *about* God. It also teaches us the mystery of God. That's another thing I love about theology: you are studying a particular

---

5 Benjamin B. Warfield, "The Religious Life of Theological Students," *The Master's Seminary Journal* 6, no. 2, Fall 1995: 181–95. This address was originally delivered at the Autumn Conference at Princeton Theological Seminary on October 4, 1911.

doctrine. You read the relevant Bible verses, under-standing what God says himself. Then you delve into what other Christians have learnt—believers who have dedicated their life's work to pursuing theology. They show you the landscape of that doctrine: its elevations, depths, beauty, and ramifi-cations. You have dug deeply into the mountain; you have unearthed mysteries upon which the whole cosmos spins. But there comes a time when you hit something majestic and can go no further. You have discovered the boundaries which you cannot go beyond. The rest is not open to you. At this point, you sink to your knees and behold God in wonder, whispering with Job, "I have uttered what I did not understand, things too won-derful for me, which I did not know" (Job 42:3). This is what makes theology an exhilarating adventure! Herman Bavinck calls it the "lifeblood" of doctrine.[6]

Could it be that the adventurous spirit inside of you—that restless longing to explore new country—was first and foremost given to you by the Creator in order that you might discover him?

---

6 Herman Bavinck, *Reformed Dogmatics*, vol. 2: God and Creation (Grand Rapids: Baker Academic, 2004), 29.

## Sherpas and Wide Oaks

As you can see, the notion that theology is a realm of convoluted mumbo jumbo written by dead guys is way off. Augustine, Calvin, Edwards, and Spurgeon are not ancient men out of touch with reality. These chaps wrote to help us understand Scripture better. Wayne Grudem rightly said, "We will attain much more depth of understanding of Scripture when we are able to study it in the company of a great number of scholars who all begin with the conviction that the Bible is completely true and absolutely authoritative."[7]

If you want to conquer a mountain, you need a guide. In theology, a person whom we might call a professional theologian is not your enemy, intentionally trying to make you feel out of your depth, naive, or in alien country. Instead, this person is your *sherpa*, native to the mountains, renowned for his or her skills. Such theologians will become your friends as you adventure into doctrine together.

In recent years of teaching women, I have seen those who had hardly touched theology before

---

7 Wayne Grudem, *Systematic Theology: An Introduction to Biblical Doctrine* (Leicester: IVP, 1994), 17.

finding the works of Herman Bavinck a thrilling adventure. If you search for images of this author, you will find a nineteenth-century Dutch theologian as austere as they come! But these women have become attached and indebted to their Dutch Victorian sherpa. He has done them a great service. Like Priscilla and Aquila did Apollos, he has sharpened their view of God and explained to them "the way of God more accurately" (Acts 18:26).

If you are someone who avoids the wordy, dusty dead guys (for whatever reason), I encourage you to just pick up a great Christian classic and crack it open! C. S. Lewis said that we are sometimes over-awed by great and ancient authors. We feel inadequate and think we will not understand them. But Lewis rightly points out it is because these authors are clear and comprehensible that they are deemed great and are still being read hundreds of years later.[8] True, some classics are wordy. But you'd be surprised. Works like Calvin's *Institutes*, Luther's *The Freedom of a Christian*, and Augustine's *Confessions* have a profound simplicity about them. That's why they are still being translated, read, and

---

8  C. S. Lewis, "Preface," in Athanasius, *On the Incarnation*, trans. John Behr (New York: St. Vladimir's Seminary Press, 2011), 11–12.

discussed. And isn't it better to read a few pages of a time-proven classic, collecting nuggets in your bucket, than to trawl a wide net of contemporary books?

Think of a good classic as a great tree, a wide oak standing tall and steadfast for many centuries, drawing many varied readers under its shade— whilst many new books (perhaps even the one you are holding) become regurgitated sawdust. We do better to stick to the ancient oaks. Their roots run deep, and they have withstood the test of time.

# DOCTRINE

*If anyone teaches a different doctrine and does not agree with the sound words of our Lord Jesus Christ and the teaching that accords with godliness, he is puffed up with conceit and understands nothing. (1 Tim. 6:3–4)*

1. Why do you think we play it safe in our reading? How can we change our habits and venture into new territory? Is there a book that you have put off reading because it seems too intimidating or archaic, but secretly you suspect it might do your soul good?

2. How would you define *theology*? And what is *doctrine*?

3. Look through the chapter again. Why do you think theology is the unique concern of the Christian?

4. What does the fullness of God's self-revelation display about his character?

5. Jesus said before his death and resurrection, "When the Spirit of truth comes, he will guide you into all the truth" (John 16:13). In what ways do you think the Spirit of Christ has guided the church in truth? In what ways are the church's historic creeds and confessions fruit of this guidance?

6. What role do other believers have to play in your Christian life as you seek to know God more? At this point in your life, who are some of the people you are learning from, and who are the people you teach?

## Chapter Three

# Robust Worship

In the grace of theology, we apprehend more of God. When we take hold of our Bibles, or books written by those sherpas guiding us through, we take hold of God, grasping more of who he is.

I started digging into doctrine twenty years ago, and I've struck gold many times as the Holy Spirit has used the Word he inspired to illuminate truth. My world was turned upside down by the doctrine of union with Christ, a gospel grace in which we behold the unimaginable beauty of Jesus. In the doctrine of adoption, I have found the Father's love believable and learnt that I have an immovable home in God's covenant family. In what theologians call "divine simplicity," I have discovered God is not a collection of parts like we are. He is not merely a superior version of humanity. He is Other—completely self-existing, unchanging, impassable.

Grasping more of God's nature in theology gives further clarity on our nature too. From Job 14 and Psalm 90, I have understood more of our frailty, teaching me to number my days (Ps. 90:12). The doctrine of justification has given me new voice as I sing of a mercy that plunged me under Christ's blood and declared me "righteous." In my understanding, God is now unimaginably bigger, and his grace unimaginably richer!

Digging into doctrine replaces vague clouds of misunderstanding and sentiment with gospel clarity. Our passion for God is enlarged as we gain a clearer, finer vision of him. In theology we know truly, to know God is to love him. What grace! What joy!

## Flimsy Worship

When I was growing up, church was all about the singing. The sermons were dull. I was at church for the music! Sure, I loved God—particularly at the song's bridge or key change. I sang my heart out, but there was so much I wasn't clear on. My worship was sentimental and superficial. My knowledge of God—the frame on which our worship hangs—was oh-so-flimsy. My faith was infantile, shaped by church culture, not biblical truth. Worse off than the

Corinthians, whom Paul calls "infants in Christ," too immature for solid food (1 Cor. 3:1–2), I was choking on milk.

Even into adulthood, my bad theology was still apparent. Believe me, it was more than the inability to fit the Sunday school stories together. I had no clue about the preexistent Christ, and for years I presumed that God the Son and God the Holy Spirit were just other forms of the Father (for lesser heresy people have been burnt at the stake!).

How many of us have belted out gospel truth from our lungs but understood so little? With only a flimsy theological frame, our doxology resounds only as tin—a shallow peal. But with maturity comes a more robust frame and a deeper ringing. And as we grow in grace, our frames grow ever stronger and stouter, so that, in time, mightier bells hang there, pealing with a richer, resonant sound.

This was true of some believers in the Scottish Highlands my family and I worshipped with recently. It was my first encounter ever with exclusive psalm-singing. Forget the drum debate; there was not an instrument in sight! But you will never be the same once you have heard Scripture belted out by Spirit-filled Scots—a potent combination. Their worship needed no smoke machines or trendy band.

They had stripped it all back; Scripture and the fire in their bellies were enough.

## Weighty Worship

One of my favourite theologians from history is an uneducated farmer's daughter who died at the age of twenty-nine. Ann Griffiths lived in rural Wales in the late eighteenth century. We know she must have read everything she could get her hands on, because she penned poems rammed full of doctrine. Writing lines of poetry was central to Ann's private worship, but now they are publicly celebrated as hymns equal to those of Isaac Watts or Charles Wesley. It is obvious from the following that Ann had an awesome grasp of theology and a deep yearning for Christ:

> O might I gain faith's insight …
> Its saving mystery;
> Two natures in one Person
> Joined indivisibly,
> True, pure and unconfounded,
> Perfect in unity.[1]

---

1 Ann Griffiths. VI. In E. Wyn James, ed., *Flame in the Mountains: Williams Pantycelyn, Ann Griffiths, and the Welsh Hymn*, trans. H. A. Hodges (Ceredigion: Y Lolfa, 2017), 175.

Ann is not interested in trite, man-centred Christianity. She doesn't write New York Bestseller material about washing your face or suggesting that Jesus called her on the phone. This young woman, living in obscurity, dug deeply and found the tri-une God:

> Earth cannot, with all its trinkets,
> Slake my longings at this hour;
> They were captured, they were widened,
> When my Jesus showed his power.
> None but he can now content me,
> He, the Incomprehensible;
> O to gaze upon his Person,
> God in man made visible.[2]

Ann is not alone. History is full of women of robust doxology. Did you know that the magnificent hymn "Before the Throne of God Above" was written by a twenty-two-year-old girl? Charitie Lees Smith (later Bancroft) was born in County Dublin in 1841 and wrote the hymn in 1863, although she named it "The Advocate." Charitie understood that Christ himself was her Priest, her Passover Lamb, her

---

2 Ann Griffiths. XIV. In James, ed., *Flame in the Mountains*, 189.

Righteousness, Safety, Justification, and Glorification. These were all truths for her to sing about!

Ann and Charitie were theologians who sung out their confessions and creeds with titanic bells. Their doxology is heavyweight because they have seen something of the magnitude of God's mercy, power, and love in theology. As we take hold of more and more of the gospel with our minds—grasping how far forgiveness in Christ extends—don't we become as the woman with the alabaster flask? Loving much because we are forgiven much (Luke 7:47).

*Where are you now, Charitie? Where are you now, Ann?* Where are the young women who in doctrine have beheld an incomprehensible God, and so worship in spirit and in truth (John 4:23–24)? Where are such women today, building up the church with their robust doxology, like Priscilla of old?

The problem is that we feast on other things...

## Dogs and Dung, or Creeds and Confessions

My three young daughters are puppy mad. They used to be so desperate for a puppy that they would spend hours crawling around the house yapping and yelping. Last year we succumbed and brought a little girl puppy home, with doleful eyes the colour of chocolate and long, velvety ears. Let's just say it has been a learning curve—not least since the day she sniffed out a place to do her business, executed her business, and then, to my complete horror, turned around and started munching on it! I screamed in revulsion! *How could she?* I soon learnt that this habit, called *coprophagia*, is common among dogs.

Not just dogs, though. Many of us have depraved appetites! We feast on the world's muck every day. We know much of it is junk—not deserving of our battery life, let alone our time. Yet we return to it, addicted. We keep on tapping, and we keep on watching, proving the precision of Jeremiah 17:9: "The heart is deceitful above all things, and desperately sick; who can understand it?" Like my puppy, we are coprophagic, filling ourselves with filth when we could be feeding on the things of God.

If our appetites were fixed on the Lord, we would say with our brother Paul that all things are "dung" compared to "the excellency of the knowledge of Christ Jesus my Lord" (Phil. 3:8, KJV). The godliest people I know are those who consume their creeds and confessions. They can't get enough of their Bibles, their churches, their meaty Christian books.

It is said that you are what you eat. I guess looking at a holy God in theology will only give you a vision which you will want to emulate (1 Pet. 1:16).

The apostle Paul had a ravenous appetite for theology and godliness. He writes to Titus in Crete, "But as for you, teach what accords with *sound* doctrine" (Titus 2:1), meaning that the Bible's teachings are true, healthy, wholesome, and safe. The root Greek word here is where we get the word "hygienic." Paul is saying that clean, hygienic doctrine produces a healthy, godly life. Our doctrine is corrupt and unhealthy if it does not touch our lives. Love for sin is "contrary to sound doctrine" (1 Tim. 1:10). In this passage Paul then says something devastating. He tells us that, as Christian women, we can "revile" (literally, "blaspheme") the Word of God by our ungodly living:

> Older women likewise are to be reverent in behavior, not slanderers or slaves to much wine. They are to teach what is good, and so train the young women to love their husbands and children, to be self-controlled, pure, working at home, kind, and submissive to their own husbands, *that the word of God may not be reviled.* (Titus 2:3–5)

Paul then pushes this further and calls for godliness amongst the Christians, so that they "may adorn the doctrine of God our Savior" (vv. 9–10). This is profound. The fruit of healthy theology is godliness. "In order for doctrine to be fruitful to us, it must overflow into our hearts, spread into our daily routines, and truly transform us within."[3] In a self-controlled, holy life, we adorn and rightly arrange our doctrine of God. This makes sense, since we are God's theologians. May we be those who beautify our theology, not blaspheme it.

## Enjoying an Inexhaustible God

The God of the Bible is infinite, ageless, eternal, incomprehensible, and unfathomable. We will never stop mining, pushing further into knowing him. The triune God—Father, Son, and Holy Spirit—is a mountain of inexhaustible riches. The rivers of gold in God and his salvation in Christ will never dry up. They are open to us every single day.

It's important not to drive a wedge between God and our enjoyment of him. We don't do this in our

---

3 John Calvin, *A Little Book on the Christian Life*, trans. Aaron Denlinger and Burk Parsons (Sanford, FL: Reformation Trust, 2017), 13.

other relationships. In my marriage, I don't separate my husband from the facts that I know about him. The quality of his voice, the mottled colour of his eyes, and the fact that he is exceedingly fond of chocolate are all wrapped up in my enjoyment of him.

Pick someone you know. Do you divide that person from the data you know about him or her? That would be very odd indeed! Isn't the word "data" in that sentence just plain wrong and uncomfortable? Our relationships are not the sum of *person* plus *data*. They are just *person*. So why do we do this with God?

Imagine provoking Benjamin Breckinridge Warfield, the American theologian, "Haven't you heard that ten minutes on your knees will give you a truer, deeper, more operative knowledge of God than ten hours over your books?" If you did, his thick eyebrows would shoot up, and he would look at you in horror:

> What! Than ten hours over your books, on your knees? Why should you turn from God when you turn to your books, or feel that you must turn from your books in order to turn to God? If learning and devotion are as

antagonistic as that, then the intellectual life is in itself accursed, and there can be no question of a religious life for a student, even of theology.[4]

For too long we have caused havoc in our own spiritual lives by divorcing God-truth from God-enjoyment. The purpose of theology is to warm the heart. Every page of every theology book exists to fan the affections into flame for Christ! Calvin says, "Doctrine is rightly received when it takes possession of the entire soul and finds a dwelling place and shelter in the most intimate affections of the heart."[5] Theology is the pursuit of worship. It should drive us to our knees in prayer and adoration. Theology devoid of worship just ain't theology!

## The Chief End of Dying Dust

I am dying. I am dying dust writing to dying dust. Scripture is blatant: we are a breath. A mist. A sigh. So let's talk about the big question mark hanging over life: *What is it all for?* Is there purpose in life's monotony, relentlessness, and angst? Maybe, like

---

4  Warfield, *Religious Life*, 182.
5  Calvin, *Christian Life*, 13.

me, you are plagued by this question when you least expect it. It suddenly rears up while you are on the bus, in the middle of a meeting, or pulling out washing from an overstuffed basket. Does the question throw you? Does its starkness tempt you to despair or to detach from life? Perhaps you wish you could take a knife to reality and peel back the incision to see what is really there?

Theology tells us the answer. The *ultimate* reality under the layers of life is the *Ultimate* himself. The *Westminster Shorter Catechism* pulls the answer to the question of our existence straight from Scripture: "Our chief end is to glorify God and enjoy Him forever."[6] We were born to glorify God and enjoy him. John Calvin says, "We are consecrated and dedicated to God to the end that we might not think, speak, meditate, or act unless it be to His glory."[7] Our breathing, sleeping, eating, washing, working— it is *all* for the glory of God. And the more we enjoy God, the more we glorify him. Britney Spears used to sing, "I was born to make you happy"[8]—which is weird, since we have never met! I think we were born

---

6  1 Corinthians 10:31 and Revelation 7:15–17.

7  Calvin, *Christian Life*, 22.

8  Britney Spears, "Born to Make You Happy," by Andreas Carlsson and Kristian Lundin, released December 6, 1999, Jive Records.

to discover God. To be his theologians. Our minds were given in order to drill into his Word and his mysteries, our affections and faculties to worship in wonder.

Yet we struggle. We want to glorify God and enjoy him, but we don't know how. Our prayer life is flat, forced, and fragmentary, and we haven't known spiritual joy for a while. Instead, we are eaten up with discontentment, anxiety, and for many of us, bouts of depression. This is often due to our theological malnourishment.

I have a hunch that whilst Priscilla suffered—facing upheaval, persecution, and even violence—she applied the realities of the gospel to her life. Her doxology was robust. She hung on to the truth of the gospel for which she lived and served. If this had not been the case, I very much doubt she would have made it to the pages of the New Testament as she did, praised by the apostle as a faithful ally.

As God's theologians, we can slake our thirst daily on the cool water of biblical truth. Let me call you to theology and to adoration—to feast upon the goodness of our God.

# WORSHIP

*But as for you, continue in what you have learned and have firmly believed, knowing from whom you learned it and how from child-hood you have been acquainted with the sacred writings, which are able to make you wise for salvation through faith in Christ Jesus.*

(2 Tim. 3:14–15)

1. How can we ensure our Christian faith is built upon biblical truth and not merely our own experience or impressions? How can we take care not to interpret Scripture to serve our own purposes or sentiments?

2. In our corporate worship, the closing doxologies of Romans and Jude are frequently read at the end of services. Read Romans 16:25–27 and Jude 24–25.

   a. What characteristics do these two doxologies share?
   b. How do the spiritual truths in each comfort you?
   c. What do they teach in relation to our doctrine of God—Father, Son, and Holy Spirit?

    d. How could you build these doxologies
      into your own worship of God?

3. In this chapter, we considered Ann Griffiths
and Charitie Lees Smith. Who are some of
your favourite characters from history with
a robust doxology? Consider or discuss
why you appreciate them.

4. How might we, as Christian women,
blaspheme our theology?

5. How can we develop more of an appetite
for God? What does it look like to enjoy God
through the study of theology?

## Chapter Four

# Sharing Great Spoil

I love a good treasure story. Give me a redis-
covered key, a tatty old map, and a legend about a
long-lost hoard of gold and gems, and I am gone
(especially if there is the further complication of a
dragon!).

When we hold Scripture in our hands, we cradle
priceless truth. The psalmist says, "I rejoice at your
word like one who finds great spoil" (Ps. 119:162).
The teachings of God are to be desired more than
gold, "even much fine gold" (Ps. 19:10). God's Word
is treasure to delight in. And it is sweet! If Priscilla
came rocking up to your midweek Bible study, I bet
she would be licking her lips, hungry for the honey
drippings of Scripture (Ps. 19:10).

We don't want to bury this treasure. We cannot
be like Achan, who in hot lust feverishly dug a hole
and hoarded away part of the Jericho booty (Josh.
7:10–26). If, with the psalmist, we do rejoice at God's
Word, then we must share the spoil! We don't want

to bury the beautiful teachings of the Bible but to build up the precious church, as Priscilla did.

We have seen in this book that as God's theologians, we must treasure Scripture and doctrine together, always learning to rightly handle the Word of truth so we can present ourselves "to God as one approved, a worker who has no need to be ashamed" (2 Tim. 2:15). We can become competent in handling doctrine so that, like Priscilla, we can "[explain] the way of God more accurately" (Acts 18:26).

## A Legacy That Shaped Another

Let's return to Priscilla and Aquila drawing alongside Apollos:

> Now a Jew named Apollos, a native of Alexandria, came to Ephesus. He was an eloquent man, competent in the Scriptures. He had been instructed in the way of the Lord. And being fervent in spirit, he spoke and taught accurately the things concerning Jesus, though he knew only the baptism of John. He began to speak boldly in the synagogue, but when Priscilla and Aquila heard him, they took him aside and explained to him the way of God more accurately. (Acts 18:24–26)

Earlier we asked why Luke, the author of Acts, would bother to include this seemingly small event in his account, especially since he is so evidently following the journeys of Paul. We find the answer in Apollos himself:

> And when [Apollos] wished to cross to Achaia, the brothers encouraged him and wrote to the disciples to welcome him. When he arrived, he greatly helped those who through grace had believed, for he powerfully refuted the Jews in public, showing by the Scriptures that the Christ was Jesus. (vv. 27–28)

Why was Priscilla and Aquila's investment in Apollos so profound? Because after his encounter with our couple, Apollos became a great evangelist and preacher. This led to the church in Ephesus recognising Apollos's giftings and recommending him to the church in Corinth. Apollos was just what the church in Corinth needed, particularly with the opposition from the Jews there. Theologian F. F. Bruce says of Apollos:

> He proved himself a tower of strength to the believers in Corinth, both by his teaching in

the church and by his preaching to those outside, especially to the Jews of Corinth, as he argued cogently (refuting all counter-argument) that the Messiah of whom the Scriptures spoke must be identified with Jesus of Nazareth.[1]

In this major city Apollos became the leading apologist and evangelist, so much so that Paul names Apollos in his letter to the Corinthians when rebuking them for their divisive favourit-ism (1 Cor. 1:11–12, 3:4–9, 21–23). "What then is Apollos? What is Paul? Servants through whom you believed, as the Lord assigned to each. I planted, Apollos watered, but God gave the growth" (1 Cor. 3:5–6). Apollos was so significant and useful to the early church that Paul unites his ministry with Apollos's: "He who plants and he who waters are one" (v. 8).

One legacy shapes another. Priscilla's legacy became entwined with that of Apollos in a way she likely never expected. Her gift to Apollos was theo-logical protection, but in some ways, her gift to the

---

1  F. F. Bruce, *The Book of the Acts* (1988; repr., Grand Rapids: Eerdmans, 1990), 360–61.

church was Apollos himself, as she and Aquila invested in and nurtured his ministry.

Isn't this what church is all about? God has given his church teachers "to equip the saints for the work of ministry, for building up the body of Christ, until we all attain to the unity of the faith and of the knowledge of the Son of God" (Eph. 4:12–13). By means of their care, Priscilla and Aquila didn't just strengthen Apollos or the believers in Corinth, but rather the whole of the body of Christ, past, present, and future. And even more so if the scholars who think Apollos wrote the book of Hebrews are right!

If the encounter of Priscilla, Aquila, and Apollos teaches us anything, it is the spiritual clout of the church community, the power of believers building one another up, "speaking the truth in love, [growing up] in every way into him who is the head, into Christ, … joined and held together by every joint," making sure "each part is working properly" (Eph. 4:15–16). This is the biblical truth of the church. We are all members of Christ's body (see 1 Corinthians 12). Body parts protect one another. If you are being attacked by a ball or a toddler, your hand jerks out to protect your face. If you are tripping, your leg jolts out to prevent your whole body from falling. Living as God's theologians means that it is our responsibility, even reflex, to protect our other members from harm and error. We build them up to sound, healthy, hygienic living by teaching sound, healthy, hygienic God-truth.

## Widen Your Vision!

Here I pause, giving you the opportunity to retort (perhaps with some emotion), "This is all very well… but I am not in a position of teacher. I am not an elder or a pastor, and I don't preach." You might even bop me on the nose for effect!

Over the last twenty years of ministry, I have met countless women who feel unfulfilled and unused in their churches. They feel overlooked as their male counterparts benefit from mentoring and grow in their gifts of teaching, leading, and preaching. Some of these women have accepted that it is not God's plan for them to preach, but they rightly feel there is more for them to do than serve drinks and cut out sheep for the Sunday school lesson. Others believe they are free to preach from the pulpit but are discouraged by so few opportunities. And many are confused and disturbed because they don't know what they believe. In short, there are a lot of frustrated women in the church. Perhaps you are one of them.

It is not my intention to get into a debate about whether or not women can or should preach. This is not the book for that. I only want us to look beyond the obvious. Without disrespecting the high office of elder and the mighty grace of preaching, I want to mobilise you to a wider vision of sharing the spoil.

Priscilla didn't need a microphone and a platform to be prized by Paul. In Romans 16, Paul names many women along with Priscilla. Did Phoebe, Junia, Maria, Tryphaena, Tryphosa, and Persis have pulpits? And yet these women were invaluable members of the church and of Paul's ministry crew. If you have a yearning to teach (and I know that this is not all of us), do you need a pulpit to utilise this gift? Priscilla didn't. There are plenty of different ways to be indispensable to the body. She shows us one, demonstrating the power of those spontaneous, life-changing one-to-one teaching opportunities. Have you found that it is often those personal and intimate discussions with a godly Christian that have greatly impacted your life?

When it comes to sharing our faith and building one another up in doctrine, we need to widen our vision. As women, we have often focused so much on what we can't do and been incapacitated as a result. Priscilla's legacy of teaching and safeguarding her brothers and sisters in Christ, remembered in her shout-outs by the apostle Paul and in Luke's narrative, helps us look beyond our contemporary infatuation with position and profile. Interestingly, not once does Paul rave in his letters about anybody's preaching or public speaking gifts. If we truly want to build a platform for Christ in the lives of other people, why are we so caught up in becoming public influencers, instead of private ones like Priscilla and Aquila?

## Plucky Priscilla versus Wimpy Women

Actively growing in knowledge of God makes us eternally useful not just to the church but to our families. Paul's encouragement to Timothy reveals the crucial role of women in passing on life-giving truth to their children: "I am reminded of your sincere faith, a faith that dwelt first in your grandmother Lois and your mother Eunice and now, I am sure, dwells in you as well" (2 Tim. 1:5). If Lois and Eunice had had weak theology, it wouldn't have done Timothy much good. John Piper once said, "Wimpy theology makes wimpy women."

> Wimpy theology simply does not give a
> woman a God that is big enough, strong

enough, wise enough, and good enough to handle the realities of life in a way that magnifies the infinite worth of Jesus Christ. ... Wimpy theology doesn't have the granite foundation of God's sovereignty or the solid steel structure of a great God-centered purpose for all things.[2]

Piper is saying that wimpy theology can never have a robust doxology. We are no good to our families with wimpy theology. And what about our husbands, if we are married women? Katie Luther was no wimpy woman—how could she have been? Once, when the "father of the Reformation" was wrestling with depression, he came home and found his wife dressed in black, looking glum in front of the fire. Recoiling in horror, Luther is said to have cried, "Oh, oh! Who is dead?"

It is said that Katie Luther turned to her husband, deadpan and resolute. "Why, have you not heard that God is dead? *My husband, Martin Luther, would never be in such a state of mind if he had a living God to trust to.*"

---

2 John Piper, "The Ultimate Meaning of True Womanhood," 2008 True Woman Conference, Chicago, IL, https://desiringgod.org/messages/the-ultimate-meaning-of-true-womanhood.

The reformer here is Katie. And she is doing what reformers do best: creatively challenging bad theology. Luther had allowed dark, dismal clouds to obscure the great reality of a living, loving God. His mighty doctrine of God had slipped from his eyes. Katie fortifies her husband in his doctrine of God and pulls him up.

What a great illustration of the fact that our lives, if built upon the solid frame of biblical God-truth, can be as hearty as the eternal realities they lean upon. Our Christian lives will only be as strong as our doctrine. Our enjoyment of God will only be as full as our gospel understanding.

## Theology Saves Lives

The world sits in spiritual poverty, and the beloved church, the body of Christ, wrestles daily against sin and darkness. We must divide the spoil. We must share the treasure of doctrine with others. *Why?* Because theology doesn't just fortify the Christian; *theology saves lives.*

You can't dig into God without hitting his gospel. As God's theologians, it is our job to be like the four leprous beggars in 2 Kings 7. In desperation, they had walked over to the enemy camp, with aching, empty bellies in a war-induced

64

famine that had turned the people to cannibalism (2 Kings 6:24–31). Yet the camp was deserted. The Lord had caused the army of the Syrians to hear the sound of chariots and horses, and they had fled.

The hungry, leprous men entered the Syrians' abandoned tents and found dinner on the table. They feasted, hoarded, and hoarded again. Then they "said to one another, 'We are not doing right. This day is a day of good news.'" They "called to the gatekeepers of the city and told them," and the people went out and "plundered the camp of the Syrians" (2 Kings 7:9–10, 16).

When we treasure theology and share the spoil, others will likewise plunder the riches of Christ and his salvation. Let's share the joy and freedom of the gospel with others. In this, our lives count for Christ.

Do you want to be fortified? Do you want the adventure of discovering more of our awesome, inexhaustible God? Do you want to be moved to your knees in wonder, growing in godliness as your vision of God grows too? Do you want to be plucky, like Priscilla and Katie? Robust, like Ann and Charitie? In dedicating ourselves to theology, we can experience a fearless love and concern for the church like that of Priscilla, fortifying the body so it can be built up in biblical strength.

My sisters, let us be women of rock-solid doctrine, Priscillas in this generation.

# TEACHING

*For though by this time you ought to be teachers, you need someone to teach you again the basic principles of the oracles of God. You need milk, not solid food, for everyone who lives on milk is unskilled in the word of righteousness, since he is a child. But solid food is for the mature.*

(Heb. 5:12–14)

1. What do you think are the "basic principles of the oracles of God" (Heb. 5:12), and how can we grow skilled in the "word of righteousness" (v. 13)?

2. In what ways can you actively share the spoil of Scripture with your friends, family, and neighbours?

3. In what ways can we shape and encourage our brothers and sisters in Christ in understanding and ministry, like Priscilla and Aquila did with Apollos?

4. Is there anything in these chapters that has transformed your understanding of knowing God? What are the next steps you will take to build on that understanding?

5. With others or on your own, spend some time thanking God for the grace of theology. Pray that he would guide you, as his theologian, to worship him—Father, Son, and Holy Spirit—in spirit and in truth (John 4:23). And ask him to show you how you can strengthen the body, his church, as you grow in this way.

# Further Resources

## Where Do I Start?

For those of you who are hungry to delve into the study of doctrine, here are ten great places to start—many of which are quoted in this book.

These resources are arranged here in the order in which they were written, but they may be read in any order. Why not start with a page a day and then pick up steam? Don't rush what you read, but chew it over. The best theologians ruminate, pray, worship, and apply.

If none of these are accessible or pique your interest, ask a pastor, mentor, or friend for recommendations. You may also want to start your own list of recommended reading for others—this is all part of sharing the spoil!

Nick Needham, ed. *Daily Readings: The Early Church Fathers*. Ross-shire, Fearn, Scotland: Christian Focus, 2017.

Augustine. *The Confessions of Saint Augustine*. Many editions are available in print and online. The translation cited above was by P. Burton. New York: Everyman's Library, 2001.

John Calvin, *A Little Book on the Christian Life*. Translated and edited by Aaron Clay Denlinger and Burk Parsons. Sanford, FL: Reformation Trust Publishers, 2017.

John Calvin, *Institutes of the Christian Religion*: *Calvin's Own "Essentials" Edition*. Translated by Robert White. Edinburgh: Banner of Truth, 2014.

*The Westminster Shorter Catechism*. This may be accessed in many places online. For a compact printed edition, see *The Shorter Catechism* (with notes by Roderick Lawson, Christian Focus, 2017). Some editions have updated spelling, punctuation, or wording.

Herman Bavinck, *Reformed Dogmatics*. 4 vols. Grand Rapids: Baker Academic, 2003–2008. There are four volumes of this great work of doctrine, but abridged versions are also available. I recommend *Our Reasonable Faith* (Eerdmans, 1956).

John Murray, *Redemption Accomplished and Applied*. Edinburgh: Banner of Truth, 1961.

A. W. Pink, *The Sovereignty of God*. Edinburgh: Banner of Truth, 1961.

Nancy Guthrie, *Even Better Than Eden: Nine Ways the Bible's Story Changes Everything About Your Story*. Wheaton, IL: Crossway, 2018.

The Good Portion, published by Christian Focus, is a series of applied and practical books written *by* women *for* women to help us delight in biblical doctrine. Current titles include *The Good Portion: Scripture* (Keri Folmar), *God* (Rebecca Stark), *Salvation* (Natalie Brand), *Christ* (Jenny Manley), and *The Church* (Erin Wheeler), and more are forthcoming.

# About the Author

Natalie Brand taught systematic and historical theology for many years at Union School of Theology and still supervises research there. She holds a Ph.D. in theology from the University of Wales, Trinity St. David, and has authored several books, including *Complementarian Spirituality: Reformed Women and Union with Christ* (Wipf and Stock, 2013) and *Prone to Wander: Grace for the Lukewarm and Apathetic* (Christian Focus, 2018). She is married to a minister and has three young daughters.

# Scripture Index

# JoyfulTheology

To download the eBook,
visit www.unionpublishing.org
and enter this promo code.

# Other Books
# by Union Publishing

*Authentic Ministry:*
*Serving from the Heart*
by Michael Reeves

*Iron Sharpens Iron:*
*Friendship and the Grace of God*
by Michael A. G. Haykin

*Right with God*
by Michael Reeves

*Come and See:*
*A History and Theology of Mission*
by Glen Scrivener & Justin Schell

# Union

# We fuel reformation in churches and lives.

Union Publishing invests in the next generation of leaders with theology that gives them a taste for a deeper knowledge of God. From books to our free online content, we are committed to producing excellent resources that will refresh, transform, and grow believers and their churches.

We want people everywhere to know, love, and enjoy God, glorifying him in everything they do. For this reason, we've collected hundreds of articles, podcasts, book chapters, and video content for our free online collection. We also produce a fresh stream of written, audio, and video resources to help you to be more fully alive in the truth, goodness, and beauty of Jesus.

*If you are hungry for reformational resources that will help you delight in God and grow in Christ, we'd love you to visit us at:*
**unionpublishing.org**